EXAMINING THE RELIGIOUS STRANDS OF ISLAMIC TERRORISTS TO ENHANCE U.S. SECURITY

The September 11, 2001 attack on the United States by nineteen radical extremist Islamic terrorists was intricately planned, calculated with extreme detail, and executed with the sole intent of attacking the United States of America and the ideals for which it stands. The principle aim of these extremists was to mount a simultaneous effort of death and destruction. This attack changed not only the U.S., but the global community at large. No other act in recent American history has elicited such a shift in the paradigm of policy and security ideology in the United States of America. Since this terrible day in our history, our people, government and the world continues to work toward defeating terrorism and the results that it brings to countries and its people.

Recent shortfalls in dealing with Islamic nations, and the wars in Iraq and Afghanistan have shown a significant gap between acknowledging and examining the religious strands that link the Islamic faith. There has been an insufficient understanding of the role that religion plays in Iraq and Afghanistan within culture, politics, society and diplomatic relations.

Within the U.S., there is seldom a link of religion or faith with the state; rather, there is a clear separation of church and state. Many times in discussions at social events or even in academic settings, most subjects are very open for dialogue with the exception of religion and politics. A lot of people just frankly do not want to discuss religion because it causes too much division, and there is the old cliché that no one can agree about anything when it comes to religion or theology. This is one of the many reasons why there are so many different denominations, religions and sects. Bible scholars have argued over centuries that a particular faith and its tenets are in fact the "one true faith". This is something that will be argued and debated for centuries to come.

In looking closely at the Islamic terrorists, one can look at the "religious link or strands" and examine some reasons why these Islamic terrorists and extremists have used religious justifications for violence, counter-insurgency, and acts of terrorism.

This paper will explore the different religious strands of the radical Islamic terrorists and how their beliefs, their culture, and societal connectivity are directly linked to their acts of death, destruction and violence. One can look at this topic of discussion and ask the question--what motivates any person or group to resort to violent acts? It is a question in conflict resolution as to why some people or groups will act violently, while others do not, even though they share similar conditions and maybe the same faith. It must be stated up front in this paper, that the vast majority of individuals that practice Islam are not terrorists, and are not associated with terrorist groups or organizations. To state this plainly--Islam itself is not a terrorist organization or religion.

However, one can acknowledge that some of these Islamic religious strands and their radical interpretations do exist, and these are directly linked to violence and death. Examining these religious strands and extreme interpretations can effectively enhance the United States' national strategy, security, both domestically and globally, and policy to ultimately achieve conflict resolution and peace.

One crucial point to begin with is to define the National Security Strategy, and Terry L. Deibel in his work entitled *Foreign Affairs Strategy: Logic for American Statecraft* states that "this can be defined as the art and science of employing and using political, economic, and psychological powers of a nation, together with its armed forces, during peace and wartime to secure national objectives."[1] One needs to come to this realization, and Deibel also states that "strategic thinking" needs to be understood, once this happens in the domestic environment it can also affect the national interests, objectives, and our international interests as well.

According to Lloyd Matthews in *Challenging the United States Symmetrically and Asymmetrically: Can America be Defeated?*, he claims that "terrorism is but one manifestation of asymmetric warfare, and changes in doctrine, strategy, and policy are needed."[2] It is very difficult for a superpower like the U.S. to begin to break through the thick layers of government, and begin to make drastic changes as a result of changing threats in terrorism. The type of warfare that these terrorist employ is one that is asymmetrical in nature, and for them, it is a 360 degree battlefield. There are no restrictions, no rules, no law of war, no humane treatment, no collateral damage assessment, and absolutely no rules of engagement. These individuals are driven to cause the maximum amount of death and destruction possible. As stated earlier, the lack of discussion of the religion of Islam and its linkage to terrorism will continue to set America back in defending the homeland against future attacks, and promoting freedom around the world.

Even within the U.S. State Department, there is not even a designated department or section that solely studies and makes recommendations to U.S. policy makers on the impact of religion in regions of conflict. Often, recommendations are made through think tanks or other contracted personnel for volatile areas that need a concentrated religious study that could directly affect an outcome of combat operations, stability or peacekeeping operations. Having an asset such as this in our State Department could dramatically enhance America's role in achieving conflict resolution in many areas. In many areas of conflict and war, religion is one the key elements that causes division.

Examining the Background of Islam and the Ideology

There are many ways to approach the study of Islam, but one way is to look at the five basic tenets of Islam, the pillars of Islam, and some of its social teachings of the Islamic faith. There are five basic tenets of Islam.

> First, there is only one God, Allah, and is creator of the whole universe, who is just, compassionate, and merciful. The absolute unity and power resides in God. He is the creator of life and death, the guide to righteous, the friend and protector of the sick and the poor. He chastises eternally the infidels to Hell, and he rewards the faithful with eternal Heaven. Second, Muhammad was the last of the great prophets. Jewish prophets and Jesus were his predecessors. Third, the Qur'an is the last of the sacred books, which include also the Torah, Psalms, and Gospels of Jesus. Fourth, the life on earth is a test and only a preparation for the eternal life to come. The "faithful" are those who adore Allah, praise the Prophet Muhammad, obey the Qur'an by doing good deeds, and fulfill the five pillars of Islam. (Note: The Qur'an forbids representation of human and animal figures. It denounces usury, games of chance, alcohol and pork. Pride is a cardinal sin.) The fifth is the final judgment, where the faithful will go to eternal Heaven, and the infidels to eternal Hell.[3]

The primary scripture of Islam is the Qur'an, and was given to the Prophet Muhammad as the literal word of God to guide all of mankind. Muhammad was a warrior when he came on the scene in Medina all of his life till he died in 632. History does reflect that when his words and declarations just did not convince people to become Muslims, he would attack them and wage war against them.

Additionally, there are five pillars in Islam, and these are followed around the world.

The first is the Profession of Faith, otherwise known as the *Shahadah*, and it is that there is only one God, Allah, and Muhammad is his prophet. The second is Prayer, and this is practiced five times a day, and on Friday's the *Salat* is practiced and this is special prayer. The third is to give Alms, and this is approximately two and one half percent of all they possess. The fourth is Fasting during the month of Ramadan, and the fifth, is a Pilgrimage to Mecca.[4]

Finally, there are five Social Teachings of Islam, and consider the following:

First, is the Brotherhood and Prejudice. The "brotherhood of Islam" is a reality, as preached by Muhammad in his "farewell pilgrimage" to Mecca, "Know ye that every Muslim is a brother to every other Muslim, and that you are now one brotherhood." This is one of the reasons why every Muslim helps the other Muslim, his neighbor, friend, or even a Muslim country. Additionally, Prejudice can be referenced in the Sura as "Believers, do not make friends with any but your own people" (Sura 3:118); "Muhammad is God's apostle. Those who follow him are ruthless to the unbelievers but merciful to one another" (Sura 48:29). Plus, the Qur'an cites Jews and the Christians as "people of the Book," mostly in a pejorative way, warning against their bad influence and life, forbidding their friendship, and calling the Jews "like a donkey laden with books" (Suras 3:60-74, 5:56, 62:5, 5:16).[5]

Second, is the teaching known as

"An eye for eye...a tooth for a tooth", and a well known passage in supporting this teaching is "Each man shall be judged only by his labors" (53:41) "As for the man or woman who is guilty of theft, cut off their hands" (Sura 5:38). Many of the "mullahs" interpret and apply this Qur'anic law, and a thief may have his hands cut off or in the case of a second theft, his legs cut off. This practice is not always adhered to in every country where Islam is practiced.[6]

The third social teaching is the teaching of

Women, Marriage and the Home. A Muslim woman is recognized by her "veil" and "chador," a robe covering the entire body, and women must be secluded, properly robed, and protected from male advantages. There is strict "segregation of the sexes" outside of the home both in the mosques, and in the streets. Polygamy is still practiced in many countries, but many Muslims insert in the marriage deed a clause by which the husband formally renounces his right to a second concurrent spouse. The younger generation leans to this practice of a marriage deed. Home is believed to be the main place for the wife, and children are indeed a blessing.[7]

The fourth is the "Holy War or Jihad. The Qur'an and the historical life of Muhammad, indeed encourage 'Holy War' or 'jihad'. The Qur'an offers Paradise to the one who dies for Allah, plus the good care of his family by God while he is in Paradise (Sura 3:169)."[8] If a warrior dies in holy war, he/she is a "martyr" and then assured a place in heaven. Lastly, is the concept of Trading and Economics. "The Qur'an, in general, blesses commerce, business, and agriculture, though it never went so far as to approve the 'capitalistic system' of free enterprise in which the marketplace, not the government, would determine the value of goods and labor. In the modern world, Islam may be nominally anti-capitalist, but the 'oil resources' in Muslim states show that the Islamic faith can embrace capitalistic enterprise with enthusiasm."[9]

These are some of the key doctrines, tenets, pillars and some key social teachings of Islam. As previously stated in this paper, there are varied Islamic teachings that are not necessarily adhered to in every practicing country, but the main doctrinal issues are practiced in almost every Islamic country globally. The people in the Philippines that adhere to the Islamic faith are vastly different than those that live in the Kingdom of Saudi Arabia or in Iran, but most countries will believe and practice the key doctrines, tenets and pillars of Islam.

Emile A. Nakhleh[10] stated in *A Necessary Engagement: Reinventing America's Relations with the Muslim World* that "Islam is a total way of life that encompasses faith, the world community, and the state, or what they call the three Ds in Arabic—*din* (faith), *dunya* (world), and *dawla* (state)."[11] He elaborated on the religious link of Islamic faith and the message of violence that is focused in several areas. Some of these messages go way back to before the Six-Day War, and eventually came to light when the Marine

Barracks were blown-up by terrorists in Lebanon, and yet can be seen in present day.

"There are some activists that maintain that Islam is the solution to their social, political

and economic ills."[12]

Dr. Patrick Sookhdeo[13] stated during his briefing at the Family Research Council in

January 2012, that the Islamist ideology or as he further defined it as the establishment

of the global political Islam is one of the main tenets of the Islamic faith.

> During World War II, the Grand Mufti of Jerusalem, Hag Amin el-Husseini was declared al-Banna's (founder of the Muslim Brotherhood) official representative, and was in charge of all of the Muslim Brotherhood activities in Palestine. He forged an alliance and linked himself with Adolf Hitler, and Nazi Germany. In addition to this linkage, he mingled anti-Semitic propaganda with quotations from the Qur'an, and called for a jihad. Additionally, Sayyid Qutb, who is regarded as the father of the modern radical Islamic groups went on to declare that the Jews had infiltrated and corrupted Islam.[14]

Dr. Sookhdeo elaborates that what developed through the years to what we observe

in present day is the modern Islamism ideology calling for a totalitarian Islamic state

under *sharia* law, and eventual world domination. "Several factors are involved in this

type of ideology: 1) The rejection of individual liberties and human rights. 2) Anti-

Semiticism. 3) The desire for the creation of the perfect society. 4) Anti-Westernism. 5)

Ruthless society. 6) Islam rules, and is never ruled."[15]

One can look at this ideology, and see it does not represent Islam in general, but it

represents the development of an ideology promoted by a particular sector of extremist

radical actors. Again, just to re-iterate that one needs to understand that not all the

people in the Middle East, the Philippines, Asia or any country who practice Islam adhere to this belief, but these are the ideologies of extremism. U.S. policy makers need to recognize this type of ideology, and once recognized and understood, they can change domestic and foreign policy to shape more dialogue and diplomatic approaches in dealing with these extremists.

Dr. Sookhdeo continued to describe this in his opinion with history and compared the Russian and U.S. stalemate during the Cold War following the conclusion of World War II with what is currently taking place in the world today in dealing with the political Islam. He referenced the stand Russia took with America when President Ronald Reagan took office, and that he adamantly opposed the Russian ideology and vowed to not only oppose it, but to defeat it. The result indeed showed the world what was behind the "Iron Curtain" and the Russian ideology with the curtain coming down and ripple effect of the freedom of nations that followed because of what President Reagan opposed and vowed to defeat.

Is there a willingness to recognize the Islamic ideology in today's society? Is there any one or a group that will stand-up and voice what is happening all over the world? Let this be perfectly clear in this paper, that Islam has every right to exist as a religion, just as the Jews have every right to have Judaism exist as a religion, and also, the Christian has every right to have Christianity exist as a religion. The message within this paper is not to deny anyone the "freedom of religion" or the "right to worship within their faith and practices". What is recognized is that extremism exists in Christianity, Judaism, Islam, and many other faith groups and sects, but one must guard in "throwing all of those following" these particular religions as being extremists. Plus, many extremists take certain portions from their prophets, teachers, founders, and sacred scriptures, and twist the teaching or scripture into to what the extremist interpretation want it to say to "justify their death and destruction".

Again, Dr. Sookhdeo states that "America is not at war with Islam's religion, however, when religion whether it is Christian, Judaism or Islam becomes an ideological and political means to an end; there is an issue worth examination."[16] This is what needs to be examined and dissected; what will the U.S. do when faced with this dilemma domestically and around the world? Plus, how will the U.S. deal with Islamic nations diplomatically? Changes need to be made strategically, and these changes could affect current policy in dealing with extremist Islamic nations. Additionally, there is a tendency with a lot of policy makers and media that will equate asking some of these "tough questions" about Islamic ideology, and the political Islam as racial or religious profiling, but one needs to look passed this and examine the "core issue" that the religion of Islam is linked as a total way of life that encompasses faith, the world community, and the state/country.

The Religious Strand of Sharia Law

Another controversial question that can be examined and worthy of study within Islam is what does the *sharia* actually mean? First of all, *sharia* does not look the same in all Muslim countries—for example, it certainly does not look the same in Saudi Arabia as compared to Turkey. For example, this can be seen in the way that women are treated in Saudi Arabia as compared to how they are treated in Turkey, and this is just one example of the differences in Islamic practicing countries. There are varied practices of *sharia* globally, but make no mistake that is practiced by some, although many may argue that it may be a minority. It also can be a strong belief by some as a social teaching of Islam or that it is a cultural preference. Whatever the case may be, it is a part of the Islamic faith, and needs to be examined and understood by U.S. policy makers.

Toni Johnson[17] and Lauren Vriens[18] explain in their article entitled *Islam: Governing Under Shia* that there are many forms of this practice and that

> *sharia*, or Islamic law, influences the legal code in most Muslim countries. A movement to allow *sharia* to govern personal status law, a set of regulations that pertain to marriage, divorce, inheritance, and custody is even expanding into the West. 'There are so many varying interpretations of what *sharia* actually means that in some places it can be incorporated into political systems relatively easily,' says Steven A. Cook, Council on Foreign Relations Senior Fellow for Middle Eastern Studies. *Sharia's* influence on both personal status law and criminal law is highly controversial. Some interpretations are used to justify cruel punishments such as amputation and stoning as well as unequal treatment of women in inheritance, dress, and independence. The debate is growing as to whether *sharia* law can coexist with secularism, democracy, or even modernity.[19]

One can continue to examine this tenet of Islam and put it to the test to eventually see, if indeed, it can co-exist in present day society, culture, to include Western culture.

The following example is a recent adherence to *sharia,* and it may well be an example of an isolated incident. After further examination of this particular tenet of Islam, one recent such example of *sharia* law that surfaced on 30 January 2012 was reported by NBC Nightly News on what transpired in 2009. There were three teenage girls that were murdered in Canada by their own father, a wealthy Afghan immigrant, and his accomplices. "The girl's father, mother, and brother were convicted of the murders and were sentenced to life in prison. What is unique in the reporting of this tragic story is truly worth mentioning as there was never a hint of referring to the term

and practice of *sharia*, but it was mentioned that they were 'honor killings', and there

was a 'patriarch cultures as men assuming the roles as owners of women'."[20]

Mohammmad Shafia murdered his daughters and his first wife and later raged about his

daughters, and he stated that "God's curse is on them for generations....There can be

no treachery, no violation more than this. They committed treason from beginning to

end. They betrayed humankind. They betrayed Islam. The superior judge in the court

case in Ontario, Robert Marenger stated that stated that this is a sick notion of honor,

and has no place in any civilized society."[21]

Robert Spencer[22] also commented on this tragic event in his article *NBC*

Whitewashes Shafia honor killing: No mention of Islam in story of girls killed because

they "betrayed Islam."

> I was not at all surprised by that, of course. Nor was I surprised when NBC's
> story aired, and it contained no mention of Islam, despite Mohammad Shafia's
> own words, but instead spoke about "patriarchal societies" and the Shafias'
> "strict religious family," and again religion unspecified. There was nothing
> surprising in NBC's coverage of the Shafia murders at all. It was just another
> example of how the mainstream media routinely whitewashes Islamic violence,
> and essentially lies to the public about the nature, extent and magnitude of that
> violence. It is no wonder that the public is thereby rendered largely clueless and
> complacent, and that Islamic honor killings are occurring with increasing
> frequency in the West, with no one daring to challenge the Muslim community
> to work against the beliefs that give rise to them.[23]

Before his conclusion of the report on the murders in Ontario, Canada on NBC Nightly

News, Kevin Tibbles stated that there really is no accurate number of "honor killings"

that take place in the U.S. and around the world because they are often mistaken as

domestic violence crimes or disguised as accidents. The evidence clearly verified that this murder was linked to the family's Islamic faith. "Police wiretaps show an unrepentant Shafia in the days before he was officially charged. Disturbingly, he can be heard saying that he would take the same actions again — even if his daughters came back to life 100 times."[24] This is an example of the extremist view of the *sharia* and again, this is only one extremist's view of what the *sharia* looks like. The point that is worthy to re-visit is what Kevin Tibbles reported before concluding his special report and this is that there is the real possibility of more of these types of killings that are just covered up.

Pamela Geller[25] cites some recent specific examples of "honor killings" around the country and has done significant research concerning this controversial topic. Muzzammil Hassan was a respected Muslim businessman in Buffalo.

> He founded the Bridges TV network several years ago to improve the image of Muslims in the United States. But now, he is standing trial for the decapitation of his estranged wife, Aasiya Zubair Hassan, in February 2009. He beheaded her at his company's office in Orchard Park, New York--that's right, in the offices of BridgesTV. Police records show that Muzzammil Hassan had abused Aasiya for years. The Muslim community there knew of Hassan's abuse.[26]

Another example is also cited in Arizona, and this case was in 2009 when a father ran over his daughter with his automobile. There was a claim of an accident, but after further research into this case the state prosecutor filed charges against the father, Faleh Almaleki.

> An Iraqi Muslim named Faleh Almaleki went on trial for murdering his daughter for being too "westernized." The Almaleki trial almost did not happen. They were negotiating a plea deal for this cold-blooded adherent to the *sharia*. But readers of my website AtlasShrugs.com called, wrote, and e-mailed, and in a huge victory for Atlas readers who fought the impending plea deal, it was withdrawn. Muslim dad Faleh Almaleki ran over his daughter, Noor Almaleki. He is now showing his utter contempt for the infidel system of jurisprudence by

saying that he ran down and murdered his daughter with his car accidentally while he was "concentrating on spitting at another woman." This disgusting defense and out-and-out lie contradicts Faleh Almaleki's own admission in November 2009 that, according to state prosecutor Stephanie Low, Faleh Almaleki admitted that he ran over his daughter on purpose.[27]

When looking at these examples, an argument can be formulated to see that this type of violence when associated with Islam is sometimes excused, overlooked by individuals or downplayed by the Islamic community. According to Pamela Geller's research, and the incident in Buffalo, New York; she believes the Muslim community knew of the abuse and "looked away". If this happens, there is indeed a risk associated with the community, towns, and cities in the U.S. However, it should be examined individually, and certainly not categorizing or making generalizations that all murders by Islamic practicing people are *sharia* killings. It also needs to be noted that this does not directly affect the national security of the U.S., but it does affect the security of local communities, and is without question is related to the issue of religious extremism.

One can ask the question, what should our policy makers do with this particular segment of a radical interpretation of Islam? They need "to hear and listen" to issues such as these and stay vigilant, by alerting this type of behavior to the local and state levels of law enforcement to look for these types of "signs and signals" in the future. Plus, the FBI can assist state and local law enforcement in a huge way by using its technology, personnel, and equipment to help prevent violent actions such as these before they happen. In many cases all across America, the FBI has been the key player in stopping terrorist actions before they are actually executed. Another valid question that can be raised is--How does one distinguish between acts committed due to radical Islam or just heinous acts by individuals? The local, state and federal law enforcement personnel will investigate these actions, and will pursue the prosecution or the dismissal of such cases. This raises another question; should any criminal act committed by someone of Islamic faith be taken as a warning sign of that faith's support of violence? Again, one needs to refer to the law enforcement for conclusions, and not assume if the individual is practicing Islam that they are extremists or that Islam is supporting violence. The key point has to be that each case is a separate case, and should be examined as such before conclusions are made.

Dr. Sookhdeo poses a very important question of what will the West do with the political Islam? He stated that "there has been a huge growth of Muslims populating Europe, and that there is a push for the *sharia* to be given official status, and finally, Western governments and the Western media do not criticize Islamism (ideology and political Islam) because they are afraid to be categorized as being 'Islamophobic'."[28] What would be different if the U.S. policy makers would examine this particular strand of Islamic religious extremism and act accordingly? The answer can be clear, that it would make our country more aware, more educated of the Islamic extremism, their radical interpretations, and their ideology. Plus, it would develop multiple avenues to anticipate and diffuse this type of extremism, and finally, it would certainly help to lessen individuals of being accused of being intolerable to the religious practice of Islam.

Examining Some Historical Strands of Islam

Observing some of the history of Islam is fascinating as one can see a clear pattern of what is documented in time and see what happened in history nearly 1300 plus years ago, and observes what has continued to present day.

Lieutenant Colonel (LTC) (Retired) Allen West was forced to retire from the Army because of some of his actions and treatment of a captured terrorist. During a combat mission in Iraq, several of his men under his command were captured by the terrorists. During this same mission, some of his soldiers within his command captured one of the Islamic terrorist and brought the individual into custody for interrogation.

Knowing that time was crucial and some of his interrogators were not getting anywhere with the captured terrorist, LTC West took matters into his own hands. He interrupted the interrogation, went into the room and demanded through an interpreter that the prisoner tell him where his captured soldiers were being taken. The captured terrorist refused, LTC West then took out his pistol, and fired a round near the prisoner. At that point, LTC West told the prisoner that the next round that he would fire would not miss. After this action, the captured terrorist said he would show where the American soldiers were being taken. LTC West's soldiers were eventually rescued, and later, someone filed a report on the incorrect handling of interrogation of the captured prisoners. Later, LTC West was forced to retire from the U. S. Army and Active Duty Service. However, the people in the state of Florida apparently looked past this set of events, and elected this retired Army soldier in November 2010 to serve as a Congressman in the 22nd Congressional District.

LTC Allen West[29] is not a "certified historian" or "scholar of history" in recognized academic circles, but what he summarized in the following remarks are indeed historical facts, and "nailed the point" of how America and our elected policy makers must understand Islamic extremists, and have to establish reachable goals and objectives to enhance U.S. security. He stated the following while campaigning for the U.S. Congress during a news interview.

> We must study who we are up against and know our enemy, because we are not fighting a religion, but it is however, a 'theo-polictical belief structure'. This belief structure has been in existence, and taking place for centuries. One just needs to ask Charles Martel in the Battle of Tours in 732, ask the men on the Venetian Fleet at Lepanto while fighting a Muslim Fleet in 1571, and just ask the Germania and Austrian Knights why they were fighting at the Austrian Gates of Vienna on 12 September 1683 as Islam seemed ready to overtake Christian Europe. Just ask why the former city of Constantinople fell in 1453, and today is known as Istanbul.
>
> You will get the answers that we as Americans need to hear by just reading the Qur'an, the Surah, and the collections of the Hadith. Upon reading these works, one will see this is not a perversion, but they are doing exactly what these books tell them to do. Until we have leaders in our nation that truly understand this, we will as a nation continue to chase our tails. One can see these marching orders outlined on any jihadist website on the internet as well. Once our nation recognizes this, our nation will have to arrive at goals and objectives to secure our republic, and also secure Western civilization.[30]

The faith, world and the state is rolled-up together for the extreme Islamic terrorist and the linkage is clearly present in their world-view and how the Islamic extremists deal with the western world, specifically the United States, our allies, and Israel. In the United States, we have "In God we trust" on our currency, on historical buildings and on some of our most coveted documents from our founding fathers, but the big difference between America and the Islamic terrorist is that Americans make the clear distinction to adhere to the separation of church and state. On the other hand, in reviewing the history in Europe, one can also observe that during the Crusades, the Christian Church and the State/Countries were joined together as Popes, Bishops, Priests, and Pastors with well meaning decrees supported the going to war and the destruction of the Muslims.

Mary Habeck[31] certainly is a "recognized scholar" at Johns Hopkins University and states that "the Qur'an and the Hadith are sources that the various jihadist groups believe they have all they need to discover the comprehensive ideology that Islam contains. The three most important ideologues of the movement, al-Banna, Mawdudi, and Qutb, provide the intellectual framework and the basic foundations for this type of Islamic ideology."[32]

Definition of terms is crucial in the study history and also in theology, and one needs to examine the terms and the meaning of Islam to really get an understanding of how the Islamic jihadist mind thinks and conducts their cause. Mary Habeck again describes that "the two terms that the extremist use for ideology is telling. The first, *'aqida* generally translates as 'religious creed', but the jihadis have re-interpreted and broadened it to mean a political or religious doctrine. Unlike Western ideologies-- political by definition--the jihadis want their *'aqida* to speak to every aspect of human existence, the personal as well as the social."[33]

It is interesting to note that the jihadis re-interpret and broaden the translations of *'aqida* for political and religious tenets for their cause. In the United States, our government takes pain staking care to separate religion and the state in policy and lawmaking. Again, Habeck describes how the Islamic faith can be dominant.

> Sayyid Qutb called the Western idea of separation between religion and the rest of life as the 'hideous schizophrenia' that would lead to the downfall of western civilization and its replacement by Islam. Religion can be a dominant master: powerful, dictating, honored and respected; ruling, not ruled, leading and not led. The other term sometimes used for ideology is *nizam* (system), and is just as expansive. Included within its scope are the economic, political, cultural, and personal spheres of human life. For the jihadis, the distinction

between religious and political, private and public, disappears, and is replaced by a vision of life unified into one whole.[34]

As recently as 1996, Osama bin Laden issued his first declaration of jihad against the U.S. "The message has three key principles: first, Islam, as a faith and territory, is under attack; second, the enemy consists of the Christian Crusaders headed by the United States, Zionists headed by Israel; and, third, jihad in all of its forms, means, and targets—including violence against innocent civilians becomes a justified duty of all Muslims."[35] These specific types of means of violence have been conducted all over the world, and then were justified like the attack on the Khobar Towers in Saudi Arabia, the attack of the USS Cole in Yemen, and the attack in Madrid, Spain on the train station to name just a few. These have been viewed as an attack or jihad against the military and civilian populations. In the Qur'an, it clearly states that suicide is forbidden, but when the *ummah* is being defended, it is then justified because of the defense of the Arab Community. This type of message and terrorism has to be identified, and that it is indeed linked to the religious faith of the Islamic terrorist. Therefore, U.S. strategies, policies and diplomacy have to be adjusted to effectively enhance the U.S security at home and abroad. This change obviously does not come quickly in the U.S. government.

Jerrold M. Post in his book entitled *The Mind of the Terrorist* states that the initial Osama bin Laden 1996 Declaration of War targeted the American military based in Saudi Arabia with the goal of getting that military out of Saudi Arabia and other Arab nations. However, in the *1998 Fatwa* there was an expansion of this declaration with the *Declaration of the World Islamic Front for Jihad against the Jews and Crusaders*, in "which all Americans, civilian and military were declared to be the enemy. The civilians became targets because they supported anti-Muslim policy, and they were killed wherever they were."[36] This declaration expanded the scope and destruction of the jihadis to enable them to target and kill innocent civilians, no matter who they are to achieve their goal. This also declared that based upon the religion of Islam that there was a mandate to disengage one's own desires and to wholeheartedly serve the desires and sovereignty that belongs to God alone. "The objective of Islam is thus to declare humanity's freedom both philosophically and in actual life. In this interpretation, Islam becomes a sort of liberation theology, designed to end oppression by human institutions and man-made laws, and return God to his rightful place as the unconditional ruler of the world."[37]

Again, Osama bin Laden stated the following from his *Jihad Against Jews and Crusaders World Islamic Front Fatwa 1998*:

> In compliance with God's order, we issue the following *fatwa* to all Muslims: The ruling to kill Americans and their allies, civilian and military is an individual duty for every Muslim who can do it in any country in which it is possible to do it, in order to liberate the al-Aqsa Mosque and the holy mosque (Mecca) from their grip, and in order for their armies to move out of all lands of Islam, defeated and unable to threaten Muslims. This is in accordance with the words of Almighty God, 'and fight all pagans all together as they fight you all together', and 'fight them until there is no more tumult or oppression, and there prevail justice and faith in God'. We with God's help call on every Muslim who believes in God and wishes to be rewarded to comply with God's order to kill Americans and plunder their money wherever, and whenever they find it.[38]

In declaring this, bin Laden is referring that God is stating this for all Muslims to execute, and he is linking what he is saying with language from the Qur'an. This is another clear example of the linkage of the Islamic religion, their interpretations with the

Islamic terrorists on their "religious mandate" to kill Americans, and their allies all over the world.

It is paramount that our American elected officials see the clear difference in our "way of life" and the extremist Islamic terrorist, as it needs to affect how they make policy for homeland security and globally. This kind of enemy knows no boundaries, and knows no borders as they seek to kill Americans and seek to destroy the freedom that we enjoy. One can very clearly see that there is no separation of the radical Islamic religion, the execution of the political Islam, and their ideologies.

Message of Islamic Extremism

Fathi Yakan[39] is one of the heads of the Syrian Muslim Brotherhood, and touches on some of the themes outlined by Mawdudi and Qutb. He argues in his seminal work, *To Be a Muslim* the following declaration.

> The *shahada* means that God alone is divine, sovereign, and the Islamic teachings and rules are comprehensive and designed by Allah to govern the affairs of man at all levels of community, from the family to the whole of the human race. Islam alone can provide the power for Muslims to liberate the oppressed peoples from the control of those who worship the false gods of modernist and postmodernist cultures. The adoption and adaptation of capitalist, socialist, communist or other manmade systems, either whole or in part, constitutes a denial of Islam, and disbelief in Allah the Lord of the worlds. Muslims in an Islamic Movement are the true servants of Allah and their obedience is only to Allah, the Almighty, in all matters of life. It encompasses not only religious affairs, but also worldly affairs. This is because Islam teaches its followers that there is no segregation or separation between religion and worldly affairs. The servitude of man means that he must reject all manmade philosophies, and systems that by nature lead mankind to submit to the false gods of materialism.[40]

What a statement for all practicing Islam around the world, and again substantiates their religion is a "way of life" for them in everything, and some radical interpretations believe that the Western life-style is certainly flawed and just flat out wrong. Plus, the separation of church/religion and state is as Qutb described will be the demise of the Western culture.

A Perspective of Islam from Some U.S. Senior Leaders

During Bill Clinton's two terms as President, he was consistent in his message on how he and his administration portrayed extremist Islam. He was careful to not link terrorism with Islamic faith. "In one of his speeches in November 1994, he commented that the American people and the West need to understand that terrorism is not inherently related to Islam, and not to the religion, and not to the culture."[41] In 1996, Robert Pelletreau, the Assistant Secretary of State stated that "extremists around the world use whatever resources they have to achieve their goals, and that a *fatwa* or incitement to violence can be just as dangerous as bombs and bullets, and clearly can be a mixture of revenge, fanaticism and the pursuit of political power."[42]

One just cannot simply deny the facts, cite this is an isolated incident or just state that this is a coincidence that there is no such "religious and faith link" to the Islamic terrorists and their acts of violence. The extremist Islamic terrorist views "the cause" being linked to the religion of Islam. The terminology of "separation of church and state" is not found in the Declaration of Independence, the Constitution or even the Bible. Through the years, the trend has been set with U.S. policy makers and the higher courts that one just cannot link politics, religion or faith together. However, the radical extremist Islamic mind does not think this way, and they do not separate their religion, politics or ideologies. They are relating their faith with their calling to defend the Islamic

Community, and believe they are "just and right" to use whatever means necessary to defend, kill, and conduct violence.

"The separation of religion and state explains for the jihadis why the West (and the United States in particular) have no moral sense: by keeping religion from influencing life, Christians and Jews have in fact destroyed the only source of ethics and morality, and therefore have no aim in life but 'to seek benefit and enjoyment'. The jihadis want nothing to do with democracy, 'man-made laws' or men legislating according to their own choices and desires."[43]

After the attacks of 9/11 on the World Trade Centre and the Pentagon, the foreign policy priority of the Bush Administration was changed and went through multiple scenarios of revisions. "The significance of the Bush Administration's policy response was to combat the root causes of radical Islam and this became the priority over immediate U.S. interests in the Persian Gulf."[44] This was seen as tightening the security of the U.S. and our allies in the region. In addition, the invasion of Afghanistan in October 2001 displayed that the removal of the Taliban was a method to alleviate a sanctuary and places for al-Qaida to train recruits. In addition, the administration wanted to move very quickly and decisively to alleviate the stronghold the Taliban had in Afghanistan. President Bush stated in his National Security Strategy 2002 that "America must stand firmly for the non-negotiable demands of human dignity: the rule of law; limits on the absolute power of the state; free speech; freedom of worship; equal justice; respect for women; religious and ethnic tolerance; and respect for private property."[45]

Scholars, "think tanks", military planners, Department of Defense employees, and many other companies are given the task to examine how Islam is linked to terrorism. In many of these terrorist organizations, there is a definite link of one's religion and the act of violence attributed to the organization. One example recently in the U.S. Army is Major Nadal Hassan, and he was directly linked to an extremist Islamic cleric, Al-Awlaki in Yemen. After the confiscation and subsequent examination of his personal computer, it was verified his ties to radical terrorists in the wake of his 2009 murderous rampage on soldiers and civilians on Fort Hood, Texas. As he carried out this terrible act of terror, he even shouted *Allah Akbar*, which means Allah (God) is great. "Al-Awlaki also exchanged up to 20 emails with Major Nadal Hassan, the killer of 13 people in the November 5, 2009 rampage at Fort Hood, Texas."[46] After this terrible event, conclusions were confirmed that he was drawn to Al-Awlaki's internet sermons, and solicited him for religious advice. Later, it was found Al-Awlaki informed the media that he didn't actually tell Hassan to carry out the murders, but he later praised him as a "hero" on his web site for murdering American soldiers who would be deploying to conduct military combat operations against Muslims. One just cannot over look that Hassan was drawn to this individual by his faith, religion and the calling to carry out this murder. In September 2011, the CIA and a U.S. joint military operation targeted Al-Awlaki, the U.S-born cleric and killed him in an air strike while he was in a convoy. This individual was clearly in the "cross-hairs" of the CIA as an al-Qaida operative in Yemen. In his remarks at Fort Myer, Virginia, President Obama called the death of this jihadist cleric a "major blow to al-Qaeda in the Arabian Peninsula, and spoke highly of the United States' successful alliance with Yemen's security forces. He also stated that this is further proof that al-Qaeda, and its affiliates will find no safe haven anywhere in the world".[47]

Is this connection between Major Hassan, and a CIA targeted al-Qaida cleric like Al-Awlaki just one isolated incident or maybe that Hassan was someone just surfing the internet during his off-duty time, and looking for spiritual guidance as he walked through his Islamic faith? Make no mistake about this tragic event; it is definitely linked to his Islamic faith and religion, and his extremist interpretation. This was not just some disgruntled Army service member, but a bold act of terrorism within the ranks of the U.S. Army. Many people in the media want to argue that this linkage just is not present in this particular case, and Hassan acted alone—try telling that to the families that are still suffering. More than two years have passed and Hassan still has not went to trial or been found guilty of his alleged crimes, and yet the victim's families continue to suffer every day in the loss of their loved ones. His trial date has tentatively been set for March 2012. Does this mean than all military members who practice Islam are potential terrorists? Absolutely, not; however, in the now required *U.S. Army Threat Awareness and Reporting Training* there are segments of this particular training to help Army personnel make a distinction on what a "threat" may look like, and the procedures to report such incidents for force protection and security "within the military". There is definitely a need in the U.S. Army for a heightened awareness of a potential threat—and the Army is briefing all personnel to be vigilant and to maintain situational awareness.

Again, one has to wonder why our State Department does not have a branch, section or even a group within its ranks that does nothing but examine the linkage of any religion of any kind with acts of terrorism or violence associated with their faith or interpretation.

The book entitled *Terrorism: The Present Threat in Context* by Stephen Sloan stated that "the line is so blurred, because to the religious fundamentalist the line between Church and State, the divine and the secular, just does not exist."[48] This line is so blurred because the faith is linked to the secular, and the terrorist will succeed in carrying out what he or she believes from Allah, the Qur'an, and Mohammed's teachings. America has to see the connectivity, and act upon this in the strategic policy toward any nation, not just Islamic nations.

Since the 9/11 attacks, Americans have flown on aircraft and some may feel paranoid, and constantly look around as if someone is going to start some trouble. There may be a legitimate "fear" of someone attacking another building, an American historical landmark, a stadium, or even another aircraft. Many times, pundits have stated in the media that one need not to equate Muslims or Islam with terrorism because this is racism or racial/religious profiling. America has to look past the racism issue and the racial/religious profiling issue and realize that the bigger issue in all of this is to protect our homeland and its citizens, and those of our global allies as well.

Peter T. King[49], the Chairman of the Homeland Security Committee gives a solid example from a hearing last year of what our U.S. policy makers are effectively executing as a result of al-Qaida's push to recruit "home-grown Americans" for Islamic radicalization. The data collected by the Homeland Security clearly displays that some of our U.S. policy makers do understand the Islamic extremism along with the radicalization they are bringing in the U.S. Additionally; they are assisting local law enforcement and empowering them to not ignore these realities, but to stop this and prosecute these individuals. The following comments were taken directly from the Committee on Homeland Security in March 2011.

Peter T. King stated that there is nothing that needs to be equated to being un-American by holding a hearing such as this one because al-Qaida is recruiting Americans within the U.S. borders to conduct terrorism. He went on to say that the U.S. Attorney General also supports this hearing and the investigations that the FBI conducts nation-wide. Plus, the Attorney General makes no apologies for the actions of the FBI and dismisses that they use entrapment or any other tactics to prosecute individuals. The threat level today is as high as it was before 9/11 because of the radicalization in the U.S. by al-Qaida. Mr. King stated clearly that the majority of Muslim Americans are outstanding citizens, but there are realities that just cannot be ignored. Even the Justice Department's own record is clear that not one terror related case in the U.S. in the last two years involved Neo-Nazi's, environmental extremists groups, citizen militant groups, or even anti-war groups.

There has been attacks in the last two years in Portland, OR, San Diego, CA, Denver, CO, Chicago, IL, Detroit, MI, Dallas, TX, Little Rock, AR, Houston, TX, Raleigh, NC, Boston, MA, Philadelphia, PA, Washington, DC, and Baltimore, MD just to name a few. He went on to state that he is asking the Muslim American Community, and its leaders to assist in rejecting this Islamic radicalization across America. He concluded his opening statement of this hearing by citing the Times Square bomber, the New York City bomber, Major Hassan, the Little Rock, AR Recruiting Center shooter, and Colleen LaRose, otherwise known as "Jihad Jane" as home-grown recruits that conducted terror or failed attempts on its own citizens.[50]

Examine some other clear and solid facts over the recent years since 9/11 from Robert Spencer's website entitled *Jihad Watch*. "Is fear of terrorists inspired by Islam irrational? There have been approximately 17,800 terrorist attacks carried out by Muslims in the name of Allah since 9/11. Would not a reasonable person be concerned about the attacks plotted and carried out by Muslims in the United States, who claim to be inspired by the Qur'an, and who regard themselves as 'holy warriors' in the jihad declared by Osama bin Laden and other Muslim fanatics?"[51] There are so many documented examples of Muslim jihadist terrorists that failed in their attempts to kill Americans inside the U.S. If the FBI and law-enforcement agencies had not had serious fears of Muslim radicals, and had not taken decisive action, some of these planned terrorist attacks would be successful attacks.

According to Carl von Clausewitz in his book *Principles of War* that "generally we are not nearly as well acquainted with the position and measures of the enemy as we assume in our plan of operations. The minute we begin carrying out our decision, a thousand doubts arise about the dangers which might develop, if we have been seriously mistaken in our plan."[52] Another military strategist, Sun Tzu stated some 2500 years ago, "to subdue the enemy without fighting is the acme of skill."[53] The past failures of the U.S., and the inability to link the religious position and the measures that this enemy will go to conduct violence and death on the U.S., even against innocent Muslim civilians, and the rest of the world has to end. Clausewitz's statement is right on the mark. There must not be a serious mistake in the U.S. plan and policy to combat Islamic terrorism by not being acquainted with the "position and measure of this kind of adaptable enemy". Islamic terrorism will continue to adapt and evolve over time. There has to be no doubt in the U.S. civilian leadership to not only see the linkage of Islamic religion and faith, but actually believe it. The logical next step is for this to actually take effect in U.S. strategy and policy making. One U.S. agency that was discussed earlier in this paper that has stepped up their efforts is the Homeland Security agency—working in concert with the FBI, state and local law enforcement.

The Post-Iraq and Afghanistan Wars

The successes of Operation Iraqi Freedom (OIF) can be seen as one observes the situation in Iraq with Saddam Hussein at the helm "before the invasion" and then examine the country "after the invasion". The country is currently conducting elections, commerce has increased, elected officials are accountable for their voting and actions in representing their constituents, and they have just started "life after the American military" since the American forces departed the country and re-deployed in late December 2011. However, there still are a myriad of problems, multiple tribal issues between the Sunni's and Shia's, and this will continue; but the people, the elected officials, and the Iraq Security Forces have to make their country succeed. The United States just simply cannot do this for the Iraqi people. People will continue to ask the question in the United States, was the war in Iraq really "worth the cost" to all of the American casualties, and the lingering effects on the military and their families?

This surely will be debated for years to come, but history and time will prove this to be true, and the shed blood of thousands of brave men and women of our U.S. military, and our U.S. allies will not be in vain. The country of Iraq is a better place with the removal of the terrorists, insurgency, and the death and destruction that they brought to this country. The "follow-on operation" currently in place with a continued large presence of U.S. government officials, government contractors, and non-governmental organizations will certainly be there to assist the Iraqi's in the re-building and shaping of their country. Contrary to popular opinion, polls, and the media, the United States will not abandon Iraq and their people, but make no mistake—the American military did exactly, and so much more what America asked them to execute in Iraq, and are still bravely executing in Afghanistan.

With the ending of combat operations in Iraq, and the combat mission in Afghanistan projected to end in the summer of 2014, what does the United States need to examine and then execute to build toward conflict resolution and ultimately peace in this region? George E. Irani[54] gives one answer to this question and states in his article on *Islamic Mediation Techniques for Middle East Conflicts* and cites the following:

> Many Middle Eastern scholars and practitioners trained in the United States have returned to their countries of origin ready to impart what they learned about Western conflict resolution techniques. In Lebanon, Jordan, Egypt, and other countries in the region, the teaching and practice of conflict resolution is still a novel phenomenon. Conflict resolution is viewed by many as a false Western panacea, a program imposed from outside and thus insensitive to indigenous problems, needs, and the political processes.[55]

This is one of the very issues that the United States faces when dealing with the Islamic mindset and especially dealing with nations that are directly linked to terrorist organizations. Doors have to be opened, colleges, universities, and also think tanks in the U.S., and all over the world need to offer opportunities for foreign students and critical thinkers to be trained, and then sent back over to their home countries to begin the difficult task of building of conflict resolution to enhance peace building.

He further explains the necessity of "the socio-economic, cultural, and anthropological background in which conflicts erupt and are managed in the Middle East. Issues such as the importance of patrilineal families; the question of ethnicity; the relevance of identity; the nature of tribal and clan solidarity; the key role of patron-client relationships; and the salience of norms concerning honor and shame need to be explored in their geographical and socio-cultural context."[56] The key is getting their own citizens trained and qualified to tackle these very difficult issues, and maintaining this over time.

In devising a plan for present and future conflict resolution, the United States has to look at key strands and study the religious connectivity that is a vital part of Islamic people and culture. Plus, the U.S. has to establish clear goals and objectives on who the enemy actually is and why they are fighting. George Irani offers more insight.

> Religious beliefs and traditions are also relevant to conflict control and reduction, including the relevant resources in Islamic law and tradition? Different causes and types of conflicts (family, community, and state conflicts) need to be considered, as do indigenous techniques and procedures, such as *wasta* (patronage-mediation) and *tahkeem* (arbitration). The rituals of *sulh* (settlement) and *musalaha* (reconciliation) are examples of Arab-Islamic culture and values and should be looked at for insight into how to approach conflict resolution in the Middle East. Finally, there is the need to consider the implications of these issues and insights for practitioners and policymakers. To what extent is an integration of Western and non-Western models of conflict reduction and reconciliation possible?[57]

Irani re-iterates the concept in his article that policy makers have to consider the implications of religion and the belief system, and this is a definite weakness of our current policymakers.

Additionally, this research is not giving the erroneous perception that the U.S. is actively shifting its policy "against those" who practice the religion of Islam. America has never stated or implemented policies against any religion. One of the most amazing foundations of America is the opportunity to choose or not to choose religion or faith and the freedom to exercise that particular religion. However, the longer the U.S. "sticks its head in the sand", and ignores the core issue of the connectivity of the Islamic religion, the belief system, and the radical ideology, the results will be the same in getting further behind in combating terrorism domestically and world-wide.

Some Paradigms to Consider

There are multiple paradigms that have been vetted and used for conflict resolution all over the world. Some have been successful and others have no success. However, one has to believe that the nation of the United States is willing to step out and make the "giant leap" and reach out to the Islamic nations to begin the phases of conflict resolution. Ultimately, there has to be some sort of compromise in resolving conflict and this can be illustrated in Jerome Segal's work entitled *Negotiating Jerusalem: How recognition of the other side's legitimacy can provide motivation for compromise.* He states that one has to be able to be willing to compromise, and in his article he dissects the Israeli and Palestinian dilemma of dividing Jerusalem. Segal[58] describes the following:

> First, regardless of whether or not people are opposed to compromise; it may be possible to get them to see that the other side does have some rights. Though not every Israeli or Palestinian will be brought to this point of view, an expanded moral discourse might well increase the number who grants the other side some legitimacy. Second, the data suggest that if people arrive at such recognition, it may indeed affect their willingness to compromise. Thus, in the effort to promote compromise on Jerusalem, it may make sense to engage right-wing Israelis in serious discourse with respect to Palestinian rights, and it may make sense to seriously engage the Palestinian mainstream in a parallel discourse with respect to Jewish rights.[59]

Getting the actors (Israelis and Palestinians) to admit to some sort of compromise is a crucial key element in beginning the process toward actually implementing conflict resolution. The key point is compromising and not forsaking ones beliefs or convictions, but working toward an agreed compromise.

One of the many successful paradigms that the U.S. Army employs is the Military

Transition Teams (MiTT), and was widely utilized in Iraq and is still used today in

Afghanistan.

> The MiTT mission is the training of Army, Air Force and Navy Non-Commissioned Officers (NCOs) and Officers to teach, coach, and advise Iraqi and Afghan security forces. After completing the 60-day training cycle, transition team members are embedded with security forces in Iraq or Afghanistan. Soldiers in MiTT training are assigned to 10 to15 man teams, and train on survival skills and tactics, individual and crew-served weapons and equipment, communications, combat lifesaver skills and cultural awareness. MiTT members receive high-quality training, and benefit from lessons learned on the battlefield.[60]

This has proven to be very successful in training the Iraqi and Afghan Security Forces

as well as Police and Security Forces within the governments in the region.

Another very successful paradigm that is used in the U.S. Army Special Operations

Command (USASOC) is Village Stability Operations (VSO) and is currently being

utilized widely in Afghanistan. These Special Operation Forces Teams have the

advantage in living and working directly with the indigenous populations over a period of

time. The same can be said of Non-Governmental Groups (NGOs) that go to a country

and live with the people and stay for a particular time period.

Colonel Robert Cassidy[61], a professor at the U.S. Naval War College believes that

> VSO are one of several national priority efforts currently conducted by joint/combined Special Operation Forces (SOF) teams in rural village areas across Afghanistan in support of the International Security Assistance Force's (ISAF's) comprehensive campaign of counterinsurgency (COIN). The ultimate goal of the COIN campaign is to foster an enduring stability for the people of Afghanistan. Performing what are commonly described as "bottom-up" stability efforts, SOF teams contribute significantly to that strategy by conducting VSO in strategically important rural areas, in villages and in village clusters, along the lines of security, governance and development, to undermine insurgent influence and control.

VSO are specifically oriented toward insurgent-controlled or contested rural areas where there exist limited or no military or police elements of the Afghan National Security Forces (ANSF). VSO enable local security and re-establish or re-empower traditional local governance mechanisms that represent the populations, such as *shuras* and *jirgas* (decision-making councils), and that promote critical local development to improve the quality of life within village communities and districts. In theory and practice, SOF efforts at the village level expand to connect village clusters upward to local district centers, while national-level governance efforts connect downward to provincial centers and then to district-level centers.[62]

Again, a small team of special operators live with the people in a specific village and they perform these specific missions in getting the people that live there back to a successful existence as a result of the effects of war and terrorists actions. This has proven to be very successful especially in a country like Afghanistan where there is little or no education, and illiteracy is an epidemic.

The development of VSO and its corollary Afghan Local Police (ALP) Program has highlighted the requirement for a national-level network to synchronize and reinforce local-to-regional successes, to manage existing civil-military complexity and to promote the efficient expansion of VSO when feasible. The district-to-national-level network assists in leveraging all available civil-military expertise and the capacity to address urgent needs in rural areas, needs which the Village Stability Platform (VSP) identify. The collaborative network extends from a national-level cell directly to regional-level cells. Regional-level collaborative cells comprise the existing VSPs and the supporting district and provincial advisory teams within the region.[63]

Many of these special operators are living in some of the most austere and difficult locations, but this a "grass roots" mission that is so crucial for the success of the Afghan people, and one that will take time and patience to achieve. You just do not see this on CNN, FOX or in the media, but has been a huge success in Afghanistan. By living with the people in the village, the culture, the religion, the lack of education, the tribal associates and many more core issues are dealt with within the village. This will take time to achieve, but has proven to be successful in the SOF Community.

Another major paradigm that needs to be discussed within this paper is what will be the U.S. role in the preparing for the end of the war in Afghanistan and establishing stability in the region. Amitai Etzioni states in his article *The National Interest: Re-thinking the Pakistan Plan* concludes the following:

> Since the war in Afghanistan started a decade ago, America and its allies have sent numerous high-powered representatives to Pakistan to cajole and pressure Islamabad to change its ways. These public lectures have been delivered by secretaries of state, foreign ministers, high-ranking military officials and special representatives (in particular, U.S. diplomat Richard Holbrooke). Military and civilian aid has been granted, and promises of more, coupled with threats to scale it back, have been made in order to compel Pakistan to mend its ways. These efforts have not all been in vain. Pakistan's military did move some of its resources from the border with India and intensified its anti-insurgency drive, especially in North Waziristan. Also, Pakistan has improved security of its nuclear facilities, and the nuclear-arms proliferation network of A. Q. Khan seems to have been deactivated. However, the total effect of all these moves has been limited. In 2011, several members of Congress called for "getting tough" with Pakistan, and others suggested a divorce.[64]

Instead of divorcing, the U.S. must make "building a diplomatic framework" one of the key elements in its plan for a Post-War Afghanistan. The lack of a concentrated effort from the State Department, and the heavy reliance on Richard Holbrooke has drastically hampered the results that are necessary for conflict resolution in this region.

Another strategy that U.S. policy makers must address is establishing a consistent dialogue with Afghanistan's neighboring countries. Major General Naveed Mukhtar[65], an Armor Officer currently commanding a Mechanized Division in Pakistan addresses this and writes in his article *Afghanistan: Alternative Futures and Their Implications* that

> the failure to establish an effective government following the removal of the Taliban established conditions for increased violence and insurgency. Governance at the local level, provincial level, and national level was always weak and ineffectual. Additionally, there was a major absence of manpower capable of providing security, and establishing conditions for effective decentralized governance capable of countering the growth of any insurgency.

Afghanistan's six immediate neighbors (China, Iran, Pakistan, Uzbekistan, Tajikistan, and Turkmenistan) and its regional partners (Russia, India, and Saudi Arabia) all have a stake in Afghanistan's future when the U.S. withdraws. It is increasingly apparent that America and its allies need to rely on these neighbors to avoid derailing the progress already made, and ideally, they will continue to support these programs when the U.S. withdraws. Such strategy requires deliberate effort to resolve regional issues that may preclude effective cooperation between the major players.[66]

One of the key points stated in Mukhtar's article is the strategy of "relying on neighbors" to assist in the progress made by the U.S. This involves diplomacy, and the time to engage the surrounding countries—this is a huge task, but one that needs not to be neglected specifically for Afghanistan to ultimately achieve stability in this region.

Major General Mukhtar concludes his article with some very tough conclusions concerning the future of Afghanistan. He states that there are five major themes that must be considered:

1.) The involvement and importance of external stakeholders. 2.) The effectiveness of the Afghan government. 3.) The capabilities of the Afghan Security Forces. 4.) The extent of ethnic divisions, the strength of the Taliban, and other insurgent forces. 5.) The will, interest and influence of the United States. The United States needs to remain constructively engaged with all stakeholders, while adopting a firm approach that dissuades regional actors from taking provocative actions to intervene in Afghanistan's internal affairs during or after the U.S. military withdrawal. The U.S. needs to employ major diplomatic measures designed to ease regional tensions, and to prevent external players from derailing the strategy. This has to happen for peace, prosperity, and stability that can be nurtured in this volatile part of the world.[67]

The key factors are the "outside actors" of Afghanistan, and how the U.S. will deal with them before the withdrawal of the NATO Forces currently deployed in Afghanistan. The U.S. State Department must get this process under way now, as the time has come and gone for planning a follow-on mission of stability or peacekeeping operations in Afghanistan. The NATO Forces and specifically American Forces will be withdrawn in

2014 following President Obama's plan for the ending of the war in Afghanistan. Additionally, given the current situation in the country as a direct result of U.S. Marines urinating on the remains of terrorists, accidently incinerating the Qur'ans, the killing of 17 civilians by U.S. Army Staff Sergeant Robert Bales, and Afghan President Hamid Karzai demanding troops withdraw from villages and return to their bases, the U.S. State Department has to act now.

Robert L. Rothstein[68] writes in his book *After the Peace: Resistance and Reconciliation* that there is a fear of peace as he discusses in his first Chapter and cites Marc Howard Ross on the following:

> The problem in attempting to resolve a conflict is not merely to seek a formula that the parties can agree, but first, find a way to alter the hostile perceptions and mutual fears that lock the parties into a zero-sum view of any proposals. Put, differently, neither psychological nor interest-based theories of conflict by themselves provide a fully adequate interpretation of any conflict, but ignoring either may also generate dangerously simplistic versions of conflict resolutions.[69]

The point made in this work is right on track as many of our current U.S. policy makers have to see the distinction of the extremist Islamic terrorist, and the people of an Islamic country.

The U.S. needs to send a clear message to the Islamic nations that they do indeed have rights and legitimacy, but also need to inform some of these same nations that harboring terrorist organizations/training camps or making declarations against the U.S. will clearly inhibit conflict resolution within their country and abroad. Second, the U.S. has to open dialogue with these nations diplomatically— there has to be a systematic and concentrated effort of dialogue opened with nations like Iran and North Korea to begin a peace process or to achieve some sort of compromise. The longer the U.S.

waits to conduct this type of dialogue internationally, the larger the gap widens and inhibits diplomatic intervention, mediation and eventual conflict resolution.

There will always be those in history who will say "it is too much of a risk for the U.S. to dialogue" with nations that are allowing or have allowed terrorist organizations within their borders. Rothstein again makes the argument that "taking any risks for peace will be difficult for weak leaders. Once it is taken, the leaders on both sides have comparable needs to widen the coalition for compromise, to produce some tangible and symbolic benefits quickly, to control and isolate the extremists, and to see the other side do the same."[70]

In Richard Connaughton's[71] work entitled *Military Intervention and Peacekeeping: The Reality,* he argues the following:

> There are three competing spectra of conflict with a wider peacekeeping model that has a wide gap between peacekeeping operations and actual war fighting. 'Peace support operations' has three distinct divisions with the first, as actual war fighting, second, peace enforcement, and the third, as peacekeeping operations. Lastly, his 'reality model' has four divisions; 1) Traditional Peacekeeping and uses Cyprus as the example with non-conflict. 2) Military and Humanitarian Intervention (short of Limited War) and uses Bosnia as the example with conflict assumed. 3) Traditional Intervention and uses the Gulf Crisis with limited war. 4) General Regional and Global War and uses the Second World War with unlimited war.[72]

Connaughton portrays these models in his first chapter called the doctrine for expeditionary conflict and elaborates by saying the "United States still has such a wealth of disposable power, and is too important, has too many unique capabilities and assets to take a back seat in the unavoidable necessity for the establishment of world order."[73] America must seize the opportunity now, and as the conclusion of the war in Afghanistan draws to a close there is an opportunity now to implement "life after combat operations" in this volatile region. Taking a backseat in establishing dialogue, ignoring key lessons learned from ten years of war, refusing to see the importance of religion and the impact on tribal issues, and not using the strategic capabilities that the U.S. possesses will create a set-back in this volatile region after the NATO mission concludes.

Seizing the opportunity is exactly what the Congress saw as a need and established the United States Institute of Peace (USIP) in Washington, D.C. There are multiple states and countries that are fragile and riddled with acts of violence, religious turmoil, and extremists occupying their borders. One of the underlying issues in the United States is that most Americans do not even stop for a moment to look at "hot spots" in the world today, because it does not affect their daily lives in some way or fashion.

Most Americans know that our nation has been in persistent combat operations for over ten plus years in two major theaters, but yet live their lives as if nothing was happening—because it just does not affect them in the daily course of their routines of life. Ask a military spouse or a parent who has lost a love one that gave the ultimate sacrifice in combat in Iraq or Afghanistan, and listen to their response on how the wars has affected their lives. Ask a military spouse and the children how their lives were affected as their Soldier, Sailor, Airmen or Marine left on a combat deployment, and was gone from their daily routine for a year or served in multiple combat tours.

Just ask the thousands of our military veterans that have been wounded in combat that have lost a limb serving our nation and fighting under our flag—for the cause of freedom for our nation and people around the world. These brave American men and women raised their right hand and cared enough about some small or large "hot spots" around the globe to answer the call of our nation and fight and win our nations wars.

One of the multiple missions and goals of the USIP is to "prevent and resolve international conflicts, promote post-conflict stability and development, increase conflict management capacity, tools, and intellectual capital worldwide by empowering others with the skills and resources, and directly engaging in global peace efforts. They also offer policy recommendations, deploy specialists to the countries, offer partnerships, grants, fellowship programs that fulfill their mandate to think, act, teach, and train."[74]

The USIP trains personnel to deploy to a region and directly engage and train the local people in diverse conflict zones. "They currently have offices in Baghdad and Kabul, whose staff work with the government officials, religious groups, women's organizations, universities, and local schools to promote reconciliation village to village. The USIP also facilitates negotiations, empowers international non-profit groups, and provides professional training and support for international peacemaking and peacekeeping operations."[75] An organization like USIP is on the cutting edge to facilitate post-conflict synchronization to enable the peace building process in areas of the world that desperately need assistance long after the military operation concludes. Additionally, the USIP is funded by the U.S. government and has a distinct advantage to assist countries in building peace. This organization needs to step up the process as Iraq begins a "new era" since the U.S. military departed in December 2011, and a bigger challenge in Afghanistan as this military operation will come to a close in 2014.

Another key paradigm in the peace building process is explained in Ho-Wong Jeong's work entitled *Peacebuilding in Post-Conflict Societies: Strategy and Process* and he cites that "while resources can be concentrated in a few priority sectors at the initial stage, a long term sustained investment of time and resources is required in societies like Bosnia, Kosovo, Somalia, and Afghanistan where the control of violence cannot be achieved without concurrent social and political aspects of peace building."[76] Additionally to the sustained investment of time, one must not set an exact timeframe for everything to take place for successful conflict resolution. Nation building just takes time and generally is open-ended, because it takes time for adversaries to address key issues and for the logistics of peace building to finally take place.

One of the largest tasks in the world now is resolving the war in Afghanistan, and facilitating the stability of this country. Lakhdar Brahimi[77] and Thomas R. Pickering[78] were Task Force co-chairs of *The Report of the Century Foundation International Task Force on Afghanistan in its Regional and Multilateral Dimensions,* and in their study they came up with several key points that needs to be addressed and eventually implemented to have success in Afghanistan. They outlined the following issues:

1) Principles to Govern the Afghan Society- Islam as basic law for the entire country has to be affirmed to guide all Afghan's identity and their society and government. 2) Human rights and the rights of women must be addressed. 3) The Justice system and accountability of crimes against humanity and war crimes needs to be addressed. 4) Maintaining security in the country with trained Afghan Security Forces. 5) Economic development has to begin with international organizations on the ground for long term success. 6) Long term management and the development of natural resources is an area that the international community can assist in establishing a self-sustaining society. 7) Capacity-building and the international community should make a multi-year commitment to support secondary, post-secondary, and vocational education. 8) Establish an interconnected regional economy, centering on natural resources, trade, and transit that will help support the sustainability of a

political settlement and will also be a gain for Afghan's neighboring countries to include India. 9) Severing the links between the Taliban and al-Qaeda. 10) Containing the threat of narcotics in the region.[79]

The U.S. has to act as the international facilitator in regards to Afghanistan and needs the support from the United Nations for conflict resolution to take place. President Karzai just does not have the capability to accomplish peace in the country alone—he must have a negotiating team behind him with the international clout. President Karzai needs to assemble this type of team for an effective outcome of the over 10 years of combat operations.

A key participator to consider in the success of this conflict resolution in Afghanistan could be the "United Nations Assistance Mission for Afghanistan (UNAMA). This organization and its members have already established a fair amount of credibility with the Afghan public, and UNAMA can provide a critical Afghan-based contribution to a broader negotiating process that involves shuttle diplomacy among various capitals, but has to remain close to the internal Afghan dynamics."[80]

Another successful paradigm can be seen in the Center for Strategic and International Studies (CSIS) Report in 2007 on *U.S. Government Engagement with Religion in Conflict-Prone Settings.* The report found the following operational obstacles that CSIS identified in U.S. engagement with religion in conflict-prone settings. "The first is U.S. government officials are often reluctant to address the issue of religion, whether in response to a secular U.S. legal and political tradition, in the context of America's Judeo-Christian image overseas, or simply because religion is perceived as too complicated or sensitive."[81]

Second, current U.S. government frameworks for approaching religion are narrow, often approaching religions as problematic or monolithic forces, overemphasizing a terrorism-focused analysis of Islam and sometimes marginalizing religion and the approach to religion is limited due to legal limitations, lack of religious expertise or training, minimal influence for religion related initiatives, and a government primarily structured to engage with other official state actors.[82]

The bottom line is that U.S. policy makers have not developed a detailed and concise guidance for addressing religion and the issues that follow abroad, and U.S. efforts have not managed to fully reduce religious risks, account for religious dynamics, and engage religious partners effectively. Misunderstanding religion can therefore lead to multiple missed opportunities. When U.S. government officials do not consider religion a factor in the success or failure of conflict mitigation, it is not incorporated into diplomatic efforts to resolve conflicts or development projects to rebuild communities.[83] One of the ripple effects of underestimating religion's role can endanger or interfere with national security and prevent the proper agencies from reaching diplomatic and development goals within a particular region.

> Perhaps the most important lesson for U.S. government practitioners is not to view religious actors and groups as monolithic entities. For example, although al- Qaeda and the Muslim Brotherhood share common ideological origins in conservative Sunni Islam, the two international movements differ extensively over politics and tactics. Merely recognizing that groups share certain religious beliefs, then, is not a detailed enough level of knowledge to predict the actions, understand the political agendas, or combat the tactics of a particular extremist religious group.[84]

Although there are some high-level diplomats that do often recognize religion's role and many individual diplomats have developed some awareness of religious dynamics while they are on the ground, the core problem is that there are no formal and mainstreamed structures that have developed to ensure that diplomats fully account for the multitude of religious factors.

42

One positive initiative was the creation of the International Religious Freedom Act (IRFA) of 1998, and this was one of the first ways religion was codified in the U.S. foreign policy.

> IRFA established the promotion of religious freedom as a U.S. foreign policy objective, mandating the creation of an Office for International Religious Freedom (IRF) in the State Department, requiring embassies to produce annual reports on religious freedom, and establishing the United States Commission on International Religious Freedom (USCIRF) to give independent policy recommendations to the President, Secretary of State, and Congress.[85]

This is at least an annual briefing that is prepared for policy makers to facilitate the process of dealing with religion and conflict all over the world. This is an excellent example of the "prescription" to increase the awareness of examining the religious strands that would enable the U.S. personnel at the embassies to make recommendations to policy makers with regard to religion and its effects. What needs to be addressed is the core problem, and this is that there are no formal and mainstreamed structures in place that has developed over a protracted two theater war to ensure that diplomats/embassies fully account for the multitude of religious factors, especially when dealing with Islamic nations.

There is a "Grand Canyon type" of separation, and a lack of coordinated and concentrated effort to establish peace with the Islamic nations. If this continues, the conflict resolution just frankly may not take place. "There is lack a clarity where those involved in protecting national security has been overwhelmed with the new roles and missions under what has been called operations other than war."[86] There should be no surprise to discover that it is very difficult to formulate a long-term strategy in a policy making vacuum. In addition, America is now gridlocked in Congress and is struggling to even change old and out dated legislation, laws, and policies within our domestic borders. The U.S. needs to reach out with renewed vigor through diplomatic means and multilateral discussions and engagements with the Islamic world to build a consensus wherever possible. This has to include partnership in the continued defense and support of peaceful Islamic governments against extremist Islamic terrorist groups and organizations.

Additionally, to support a more articulated role of religion in the U. S. national security policy, military commanders should consider ways to include religion in their campaign design and planning. This would help in dealing with the different tribal differences especially in Afghanistan. Planning with religion in mind will help military commanders on the ground get a better grasp and understanding of the actual environment, acknowledge multiple complex problems, and help create opportunities to provide enduring solutions in a combat environment.

The current 112th Congress has major difficulty approving any new policies, while the terrorist's strategy is clear; that is to continue to plan, and wait for the right time to strike again. "Terrorism has been viewed as a form of protracted warfare, and the terrorist who engages in asymmetric warfare against a greatly superior power has time on his side."[87] These facts must affect our policy makers, their approved policies and the implemented strategies that will follow. Taking these facts into consideration, will enhance the U.S. security within the fifty states, will enhance security in dealing with terrorists abroad, and will help the long and difficult process of eventual conflict resolution with Islamic nations and nations all over the world.

Without question, this subject matter will be debated and argued for many years to come. Within this research paper, there is clear and substantiated evidence of the Islamic religious strands and linkage to its extremists, radical militant groups, terrorist groups, the execution of their violence, and their global political ideology. The inability of U.S. policymakers to see this religious linkage, and the failure to apply the lessons learned to continue to effect positive change with Islamic nations will result in America "looking on the outside" in regards to achieving conflict resolution. The U.S. must have a clear vision, objectives and attainable goals in dealing with Islamic extremists. Plus, it must not just divorce itself from addressing the problems by just "kicking the can down the road", and adhering to the same outdated strategies and policies. America must address Islamic extremism and radicalization by examining the connectivity and strands of its religion, and its ideology. The result will be a stronger America, united to defeat terrorism, and become a vital peace building actor for Islamic nations.

Endnotes:

[1] Terry L. Deibel, *Foreign Affairs Strategy: Logic for American Statecraft,* (Cambridge and New York: Cambridge Press), 2007, 7.

[2] Lloyd Matthews, editor, *Challenging the United States Symmetrically and Asymmetrically: Can America be Defeated?* (Carlisle Barracks, PA: Strategic Studies Institute, 1998), 190-191.

[3] The Bohemian Guide to faith. Listings of Multiple Faiths. http://www.religion-spirituality.org/islam/doctrines-tenets.php (accessed March 13, 2012).

[4] Ibid

[5] Ibid.

[6] Ibid.

[7] Ibid.

[8] Ibid.

[9] Ibid.

[10] Emile A. Nakhleh, Prior to joining the CIA, Nakhleh was professor and department chair at Mount St. Mary's University. He was previously a Fulbright senior research fellow in Bahrain and Jerusalem, a visiting professor at Bir Zeit University, a Woodrow Wilson guest scholar, and a National Endowment for the Humanities research fellow. He has written over 30 scholarly journal articles and is the author of numerous books, including *A Necessary Engagement: Reinventing America's Relations with the Muslim World* (2009); *Bahrain: Political Development in a Modernizing Society* (1976); *The Gulf Cooperation Council: Policies, Problems, and Prospects* (1986); and *The Persian Gulf and American Policy* (1982). Nakhleh holds a Ph.D. in international relations from American University, an M.A. in political science from Georgetown University, and a B.A. in political science from Saint John's University, Minnesota (Political Science, 1963).

[11] Emile A. Nakhleh, A *Necessary Engagement: Reinventing America's Relations with the Muslim World* (Princeton and Oxford: Princeton University Press, 2009), 4.

[12] Ibid.

[13] Patrick Sookhdeo is the director of the Institute for the Study of Islam and Christianity, a Christian research institute specializing in the status of Christian minorities in the Muslim world. He is also international director of the Barnabas Fund. Dr. Sookhdeo is a prolific lecturer and author and holds a Ph.D. from London University's School of Oriental and African Studies and a D.D. from Western Seminary, Oregon. In 2001, Dr. Sookhdeo was awarded the Coventry Cathedral International Prize for Peace and Reconciliation, and in 1990, he was given the Templeton Project Trust prize for progress in religion.

[14] Dr. Patrick Sookhdeo, Family Research Council, January 26, 2012, http://www.frc.org/events/Responding to Islam: Lessons Learned from Dietrich Bonhoffer, Karl Barth, and Bishop George Bell (accessed February 1, 2012).

[15] Ibid.

[16] Ibid.

[17] Toni Johnson has spent the majority of her journalism career devoted to covering U.S. policy. Ms. Johnson spent four years as a reporter for *Congressional Quarterly* where she covered a range of legislation, including bills for energy, environment, technology, and water and highway infrastructure. Prior to that, she worked at Washington's *Federal Paper* where she covered the Education Department and small federal agencies. She received her undergraduate degree from Simon's Rock College of Bard in arts and aesthetics and her masters in international journalism from American University. In 2009, she was selected to travel to Peru as

a Gatekeeper Editor by the International Reporting Project at Johns Hopkins University. She also was selected for the East West Center's Senior Journalists Seminar and in 2010 traveled to India and Malaysia to discuss bridging the gap between the United States and Muslims in the region.

[18] Lauren Vriens is a Fulbright Fellow in Bahrain researching human capital development initiatives of the government. In 2010, she was a Critical Language Enhancement Scholar in Cairo. She graduated from the Macaulay Honors College at Hunter College in May 2010 with a BA in Political Science and Arabic. During undergrad, she interned at both the Council on Foreign Relations and the U.S. Embassy in Bahrain.

[19] Toni Johnson and Lauren Vriens, *Islam: Governing Under Sharia*, October 24, 2011, http://www.cfr.org/religion/islam-governing-under-sharia/p8034 (accessed February 2, 2012).

[20] Kevin Tibbles, NBC Nightly News MSNBC.com Video, January 30, 2012, http://www.jihadwatch.org/2012/02/post-4html, (accessed February 5, 2012).

[21] Ibid.

[22] Robert Spencer is the director of Jihad Watch, a program of the David Horowitz Freedom Center, and the author of ten books, including two *New York Times* bestsellers, *The Truth About Muhammad* and *The Politically Incorrect Guide to Islam (and the Crusades)*. His latest book is *Did Muhammad Exist? An Inquiry Into Islam's Obscure Origins* (ISI), coming in April 2012. Spencer has led seminars on Islam and jihad for the United States Central Command, United States Army Command and General Staff College, the U.S. Army's Asymmetric Warfare Group, the FBI, the Joint Terrorism Task Force, and the U.S. intelligence community. Spencer (MA, Religious Studies, University of North Carolina at Chapel Hill) has been studying Islamic theology, law, and history in depth since 1980. As an Adjunct Fellow with the Free Congress Foundation in 2002 and 2003, he wrote a series of monographs on Islam: *An Introduction to the Qur'an*; *Women and Islam*; *An Islamic Primer*; *Islam and the West*; *The Islamic Disinformation Lobby*; *Islam vs. Christianity*; and *Jihad in Context*. More recently he has also written monographs for the David Horowitz Freedom Center: *Islamophobia: Thought Crime of the Totalitarian Future* (with David Horowitz); *Obama and Islam* (with David Horowitz); *What Americans Need to Know About Jihad*; *The Violent Oppression of Women in Islam* (with Phyllis Chesler); *Islamic Leaders' Plan for Genocide*; and *Muslim Persecution of Christians*.

[23] Ibid.

[24] Billy Hallowell, The Blaze, November 16, 2011, *'Honor Killing': Muslim Father Charged With Daughters' Murder Said He'd Do it Again…100 Times*, http://www.theblaze.com/stories/honor-killing-muslim-father-charged-with-daughters-deaths-said-hed-do-it-again-100-times/, (accessed February 05, 2012).

[25] Pamela Geller is the founder, editor and publisher of Atlas Shrugs.com and executive director of the American Freedom Defense Initiative (AFDI) and Stop Islamization of America

(SIOA). She is the author of Stop the Islamization of America: A Practical Guide to the Resistance (WND Books) and The Post-American Presidency: The Obama Administration's War on America with Robert Spencer (foreword by Ambassador John Bolton), (Simon & Schuster). She is also a regular columnist for World Net Daily, Andrew Breitbart's Big Government and Big Journalism, the American Thinker, and other publications. Pamela Geller received the Annie Taylor Award for Courage in 2010 from the David Horowitz Freedom Center. In October 2011, the United States Marine Corps presented her with the flag flown on September 11, 2011 over Camp Leatherneck, "amid the battlefields of Afghanistan during decisive operations against enemy forces in Helmand Province." She has broken numerous important stories -- notably the questionable and illegal foreign sources of some of the financing of the Obama campaign, the anti-Semitic posts on Obama's website, Obama's political organizing in public school classrooms, ACORN's destruction of Republican voter registrations, and many more, but perhaps she is best known for her leadership against the Ground Zero mosque.

[26] Pamela Geller, *Honor Killing in America*, January 27, 2011, http://www.americanthinker.com/2011/01/honor_killing_in_america.html, (accessed February 15, 2012).

[27] Ibid.

[28] Dr. Patrick Sookhdeo, Family Research Council, January 26, 2012, http://www.frc.org/events/Responding to Islam: Lessons Learned from Dietrich Bonhoffer, Karl Barth, and Bishop George Bell (accessed February 1, 2012).

[29] Congressman Allen West received his Bachelor's degree while on an ROTC scholarship at the University of Tennessee, and later went on to get a Master's degree from Kansas State University, both in political science. He also holds a Master of Military Arts and Sciences from the U.S. Army Command and General Staff Officer College in political theory and military operations. In 2004, after serving 22 years in the Army, West retired from the Military, and brought his wife, Angela, and two daughters, Aubrey and Austen, to South Florida, to be closer to his wife's family. In November of 2010, Congressman West was honored to be able to continue his oath of service to his country, when he was elected to be a Representative in the Congress of the United States.

[30] LTC Allen West, American Family Association, November 9, 2010. *You Tube*, video file, http://secure.afa.net/afa/activism/takeaction.asp?id=384 (accessed January 11, 2012).

[31] Mary Habeck, she is the Associate Professor of Strategic Studies at Johns Hopkins University and held appointment at the National Security Council; served as associate professor of history at Yale University; coordinated the Yale Russian Archive Project to facilitate access to documents in the former Soviet archives; Ph.D., history, Yale University. Some of her publications are *Attacking America: How Jihadis Are Fighting Their 200-Year War With the U.S.* (forthcoming 2011); *Knowing the Enemy: Jihadist Ideology and the War on Terror* (2006); *Storm of Steel: The Development of Armor Doctrine in Germany and the Soviet Union, 1919-1939* (2003); *Spain Betrayed: The Soviet Union in the Spanish Civil War*, co-editor (2001); *The Great War and the Twentieth Century*, co-editor (2000); *Oxford Essential Dictionary of the U.S.*

Military, consultant (2001); contributed to the *Journal of Military History, The International History Review, The Journal of Modern History* and other journals.

[32] Mary Habeck, *Knowing the Enemy (New* Haven & London: Yale University Press, 2006), 57.

[33] Ibid., 57-58.

[34] Ibid., 58.

[35] Ibid., 13.

[36] Jerrold M. Post, *The Mind of the Terrorist* (New York: Palgrave Macmillan Press, 2007), 198.

[37] Mary Habeck, *Knowing the Enemy (New* Haven & London: Yale University Press, 2006), 62.

[38] Jerrold M. Post, *The Mind of the Terrorist* (New York: Palgrave Macmillan Press, 2007), 198.

[39] Fathi Yakan was a prominent Islamic scholar and caller. He was born in Tripoli, north of Lebanon, on the 9th of February 1933. With a Ph.D. in Arabic and Islamic Studies, Sheikh Yakan was among the pioneers of the Islamic movement in the 1950s. He was also the General Secretary of the Lebanese Al-Jamaa Al-Islamiya from 1962 until 1992 when he won his seat in the Lebanese parliament. He was key activist on the political stage, which was very clear during the 1996 elections. The Islamic scholar also played a significant role in mending fences between political parties in the region. He was the mediator between the Islamic brotherhood in Syria and President Bachar Assad. He also played the same role between Syria and Turkey between 1998 and 1999, in the wake of the Syria-Turkey crisis. He is the author of more than 35 books; some of them were translated into many languages, including*: How do we call for Islam? Towards a unified global Islamic Movement.*

[40]Mary Habeck, *Knowing the Enemy (New* Haven & London: Yale University Press, 2006), 68-69.

[41] Steven Wright, *The United States and the Persian Gulf Security* (United Kingdom: Ithaca Press, 2007), 70.

[42] Ibid., 73.

[43] Mary Habeck, *Knowing the Enemy (New* Haven & London: Yale University Press, 2006), 72-73.

[44] Ibid., 81-82.

[45] *The National Security Strategy of the United States of America*, September 17, 2002, Chapter 2, page 9, http://georgewbush-whitehouse.archives.gov/nsc/nss/2002/nss.pdf, (accessed February 15, 2012).

[46] Robert Spencer, *Al-Awliki the Dead Terrorist,* 30 September 2011, http://jihadwatch.org/2011/09 (accessed October 4, 2011).

[47] CBS News, *Al Qaeda's Anwar al-Awlaki killed in Yemen*, September 30, 2011, http://www.cbsnews.com/2100-202_162-20113732.html (accessed March 21, 2012).

[48] Stephen Sloan, *Terrorism: The Present Threat in Context* (Oxford/New York: Berg Publishers, 2006), 21-22.

[49] Peter T. King is serving his tenth term in the U.S. House of Representatives. Rep. King is Chairman of the Homeland Security Committee and also serves on the Financial Services Committee and Permanent Select Committee on Intelligence. Congressman King has been a leader in the ongoing effort to have Homeland Security funding based on threat analysis and is a strong supporter of the war against international terrorism, both at home and abroad. As Chairman of the Homeland Security Committee, he has stood up to the pressure from special interest groups and the media to hold a series of hearings on Islamic radicalization. Chairman King has led the fight to continue funding to the Secure the Cities Program to protect the New York-Long Island region from nuclear dirty bomb attacks. Peter T. King was born on April 5, 1944, is a graduate of St. Francis College, Brooklyn, and the University of Notre Dame Law School. He is a lifelong resident of New York and has lived in Nassau County for more than 40 years.

[50] Peter T. King, *Committee on Homeland Security will hold a hearing entitled "The Extent of Radicalization in the American Muslim Community and that Community's Response.",* March 10, 2011, http://homeland.house.gov/hearing/hearing-%E2%80%9C-extent-radicalization-american-muslim-community-and-communitys-response%E2%80%9D (accessed February 12, 2012).

[51] Robert Spencer, Spencer *and Horowitz in National Review: The term "Islamophobia" is designed to Create Modern-day Thought Crime,* 30 September 2011, http://jihadwaitch.org/2011/09 (accessed October 11, 2011).

[52] Hans W. Gatzke editor, *Part IV, Applications of These Principles in Time of War #1,* September 1942, http://Clausewitz.com (accessed October 14, 2011).

[53] Terry L. Deibel, *Foreign Affairs Strategy* (Cambridge, New York: Cambridge University Press, 2007), 6.

[54] George E. Irani is a Visiting Assistant Professor in Political Science at Washington College. Between 1993 and 1997, he was a faculty member in Political Science at the Lebanese American University (formerly Beirut University College, where he taught courses on conflict

resolution, and was one of the founders of the Lebanese Conflict Resolution Network (LCRN). In 1997-1998, he was a Jennings Randolph Senior Fellow at the U.S. Institute of Peace.

[55] George E. Irani, *Islamic Mediation Techniques for Middle East Conflicts,* Middle East Review of International Affairs Journal, Volume 3, No.2, June 1999, http://meria.idc.ac.il/journal/1999/issue2/jv3n2a1.html (accessed January 10, 2012).

[56] Ibid.

[57] Ibid.

[58] Jerome Segal is a Senior Research Scholar at the Center for International and Strategic Studies as well as a Research Scholar at the Institute for Philosophy and Public Policy at the University of Maryland. In addition, he is President and founder of The Jewish Peace Lobby. Initially trained as a philosopher, Dr. Segal received his Ph.D. from the University of Michigan. He taught for several years in the Philosophy Department of the University of Pennsylvania. He then returned to school, and received an MPA from the Hubert Humphrey School of Public Affairs (University of Minnesota). Since 1982 he has been active in the American Jewish peace movement. In the spring of 1987, he was part of the first American Jewish delegation to meet with the PLO leadership (then in Tunis). During 1988, he played a role in the events leading up to the opening of the U.S. and PLO dialogue in December 1988. Earlier that year his essays in Palestinian and American papers played a catalytic role in the PLO's decision to issue a Declaration of Independence and launch a unilateral peace initiative. In 1989, he started the Jewish Peace Lobby, which is now an organization of roughly 4500 people including some 400 rabbis.

[59] Jerome Segal, *Negotiating Jerusalem-How Recognition of the Other Side's Legitimacy can Provide Motivation for Compromise,* Palestine-Israel Journal, Volume 4, Nos. 3 & 4, 1997, http://www.pij.org/details.php?id=460 (accessed January 10, 2012).

[60] Shania Howard, 1st Infantry Division, Fort Riley, KS, Public Affairs, *Army Secretary Views MiTT Training at Fort Riley, Kansas, November 3, 2006,* http://www.army.mil/article/501/Army_Secretary_views_MiTT_training_at_Fort_Riley/ (accessed February 6, 2012).

[61] Robert Cassidy is a military professor at the Naval War College and is a member of the Royal United Services Institute Advisory Board. He earned his Ph.D. from the Fletcher School, where he concentrated in strategy, security studies, and international law. Cassidy has master's degrees in international relations, diplomacy, and strategy from Boston University, the Fletcher School of Law and Diplomacy, and the Naval War College. He has the Diplôme d'Études Supérieures de Défense from the French Joint Defense College. Colonel Cassidy has served in a variety of organizations as a special operations strategic planner, a battalion commander, a special assistant to two senior generals, a brigade operations officer, a divisional cavalry executive officer, an airborne air cavalry troop commander, a support platoon leader, and a scout platoon leader. He also served as an assistant professor of international relations at West Point and as an NCO interrogator in the 82nd Airborne Division. Colonel Cassidy has

served on several operational deployments, to Iraq, Afghanistan, the Persian Gulf, Egypt, and Grenada. He most recently served as the special assistant to the commander of ISAF Joint Command in Afghanistan from June 2010 to June 2011.

[62] Colonel Ty Connett and Colonel Robert Cassidy, U.S. Army Special Warfare Center Magazine, *Village Stability Operations: More Than Village Defense, July-September 2011 edition,* http://www.soc.mil/swcs/swmag/archive/SW2403/SW2403VillageStabilityOperations_MoreThan VillageDefense.html (accessed February 6, 2012).

[63] Ibid.

[64] Amitai Etzioni, The National Interest, *Rethinking the Pakistan Plan,* January 4, 2012, http://nationalinterest.org/article/rethinking-the-pakistan-plan-6285, (accessed February 5, 2012).

[65] Naveed Mukhtar is an Armor Officer currently commanding a Mechanized Division in Pakistan. He is a graduate of Pakistan Military Academy; Ecole D' Application De L' Arme Blindee Et De La Cavalerie, France; Command and Staff College, Pakistan; Joint Command and Staff College, Philippines; National Defense University, Pakistan; and the United States Army War College (USAWC). He also holds two master degrees in War Studies and Strategic Studies. General Naveed has served in a variety of command and staff positions at nearly every level during peace and conflict.

[66] Major General Naveed Mukhtar, *Afghanistan: Alternative Futures and Their Implications,* Parameters: U.S. Army War College Quarterly, Volume XLI, No. 2, Summer 2011, 63-64.

[67] Ibid., 73.

[68] Robert L. Rothstein is Harvey Picker Professor of International Relations and Professor of Political Science. He holds a Ph. D. from Columbia University, has contributed to numerous scholarly journals, and is author of eight books including Global Bargaining and the forthcoming In Fear of Peace: Resistance and Reconciliation in Resolving Protracted Conflict. Professor Rothstein has been a Fellow at the U.S. Institute of Peace, Carnegie Foundation, and Woodrow Wilson International Center for Scholars, and the Ford Foundation, and has served as a consultant to the U.S. Department of State and the United Nations. His research focus is international political economy.

[69] Robert L. Rothstein, editor, *After the Peace: Resistance and Reconciliation* (Boulder/London: Lynne Rienner Publishers, 1999), 18.

[70] Ibid., 19.

[71] Richard Connaughton, acknowledging that the development of today's international collective security system has been largely ad hoc and conditioned by a multitude of diverse interests, Richard Connaughton's groundbreaking investigation uncouples present arrangements by re-examining the early philosophies and the development of international organizations. Drawing on practical experience, Connaughton assesses the fundamentals which impinge upon today's regime of disorder, identifying new definitions, principles and key factors which influence decision making processes. In support of these conclusions, the book features detailed case studies of Iraq, Somalia, Rwanda, Kosovo, East Timor and Sierra Leone. This realistic view of military intervention and peacekeeping provides a new perspective which promises a more rewarding future for the international security system. This is essential reading academics and practitioners of international relations and conflict management. "Military Intervention and Peacekeeping: The Reality" has received independent recognition by being short-listed for the Westminster Medal for Military Literature 2002.

[72] Richard Connaughton, *Military Intervention and Peacekeeping: The Reality* (Hampshire, England: Ashgate Publishing, 2001), 51.

[73] Ibid., 33.

[74] United States Institute of Peace, *Fact Sheet* (Washington, D.C.: USIP Public Affairs and Communications, 2010), 1.

[75] Ibid.

[76] Ho-Wong Jeong, *Peacebuilding in Postconflict Societies: Strategy and Process* (Boulder/London: Lynne Rienner Publishers, 2005), 27.

[77] Lakhdar Brahimi, Ambassador Brahimi was appointed Special Adviser to the Secretary-General on 1 January 2004. As Special Adviser, Mr. Brahimi advises the Secretary-General on a wide range of issues, including situations in the areas of conflict prevention and conflict resolution. He is a former Special Representative of the Secretary-General for Afghanistan and Head of the United Nations Assistance Mission in Afghanistan (from 3 October 2001 to 31 December 2004). Ambassador Brahimi was entrusted with overall authority for the political, human rights, relief, and recovery and reconstruction activities of the United Nations in Afghanistan. Mr. Brahimi previously served as the Secretary-General's Special Envoy for Afghanistan from July 1997 until October 1999. In between his Afghanistan assignments, Mr. Brahimi served as Under-Secretary-General for Special Assignments in Support of the Secretary-General's Preventive and Peacemaking efforts. In this capacity, he chaired an independent panel established by Secretary-General Annan to review United Nations peace operations. Prior to his first Afghanistan appointment, Mr. Brahimi served as Special Representative for Haiti (from 1994 to 1996), and Special Representative for South Africa (from December 1993 to June 1994). In the latter position, he led the United Nations Observer Mission until the 1994 democratic elections that resulted in Nelson Mandela taking the presidency of post-apartheid South Africa. He has also undertaken special missions on behalf of the Secretary-General to a number of countries, including Zaire (now the Democratic Republic of the Congo), Yemen, Liberia, Nigeria and Sudan.

[78] Thomas R. Pickering, Ambassador Pickering is vice chairman of Hills & Company, an international consulting firm providing advice to U.S. businesses on investment, trade, and risk assessment issues abroad, particularly in emerging market economies. He retired in 2006 as senior vice president international relations for Boeing. He has had a career spanning five decades as a U.S. diplomat, serving as Under Secretary of State for political affairs, ambassador to the United Nations, ambassador to Russia, India, Israel, Nigeria, Jordan and El Salvador. He also served on assignments in Zanzibar and Dar es Salaam, Tanzania. He holds the personal rank of Career Ambassador, the highest in the U.S. Foreign Service. He has held numerous other positions at the State Department, including executive secretary and special assistant to Secretaries Rogers and Kissinger and assistant secretary for the bureau of oceans, environmental and scientific affairs. He is based in Washington, DC.

[79] Lakhdar Brahimi and Thomas R. Pickering, *Afghanistan: Negotiating Peace* (New York: The Century Foundation Press, 2011), 32-43.

[80] Ibid., 57-58.

[81] Lior Danan and Alice Hunt, The Center for Strategic and International Studies, *Mixed Blessings: U.S. Government Engagements with Religion in Conflict Prone Settings,* (Washington, D.C.: The CSIS Press, 2007), 3.

[82] Ibid.

[83] Ibid., 6.

[84] Ibid., 7.

[85] Ibid., 11.

[86]Lloyd Matthews, editor, *Challenging the United States Symmetrically and Asymmetrically: Can America be Defeated?* (Carlisle Barracks, PA: Strategic Studies Institute, 1998), 188.

[87] Ibid., 189.